A HOUSE

KEVIN HENKES

GREENWILLOW BOOKS
An Imprint of HarperCollinsPublishers

A HOUSE

For L, W, C & S

A House. Copyright © 2021 by Kevin Henkes. All rights reserved. Printed in the United States of America. For information address HarperCollins Children's Books, a division of HarperCollins Publishers, 195 Broadway, New York, NY 10007. www.harpercollinschildrens.com. Brown ink, watercolor paint, and colored pencils were used to prepare the full-color art. The text type is 28-point Memphis Medium. Library of Congress Cataloging-in-Publication Data is available. ISBN 9780063092600 (hardback) | ISBN 9780063092617 (lib. bdg.) 21 22 23 24 25 WOR 10 9 8 7 6 5 4 3 2 1 First Edition. Greenwillow Books

A house.

Where is the door?

What color is it?

Where is the window?

What shape is it?

A house

in the morning.

Where is the sun?

Is it up?

Where are the birds?

Are all of them flying?

A house

at night.

Where is the moon?

Does it look like the window?

Where are the stars?

How many are there?

A house

in the rain.

Where are the clouds?

Which one is smallest?

Where are the puddles?

Which one is biggest?

A house

in the snow.

So much snow!

Where is the house?

A house.

Look!

Here comes a dog.

Here comes a cat.

Here come some people.

What are they doing?

They are coming home.

A home.